The DECLARATION of INDEPENDENCE

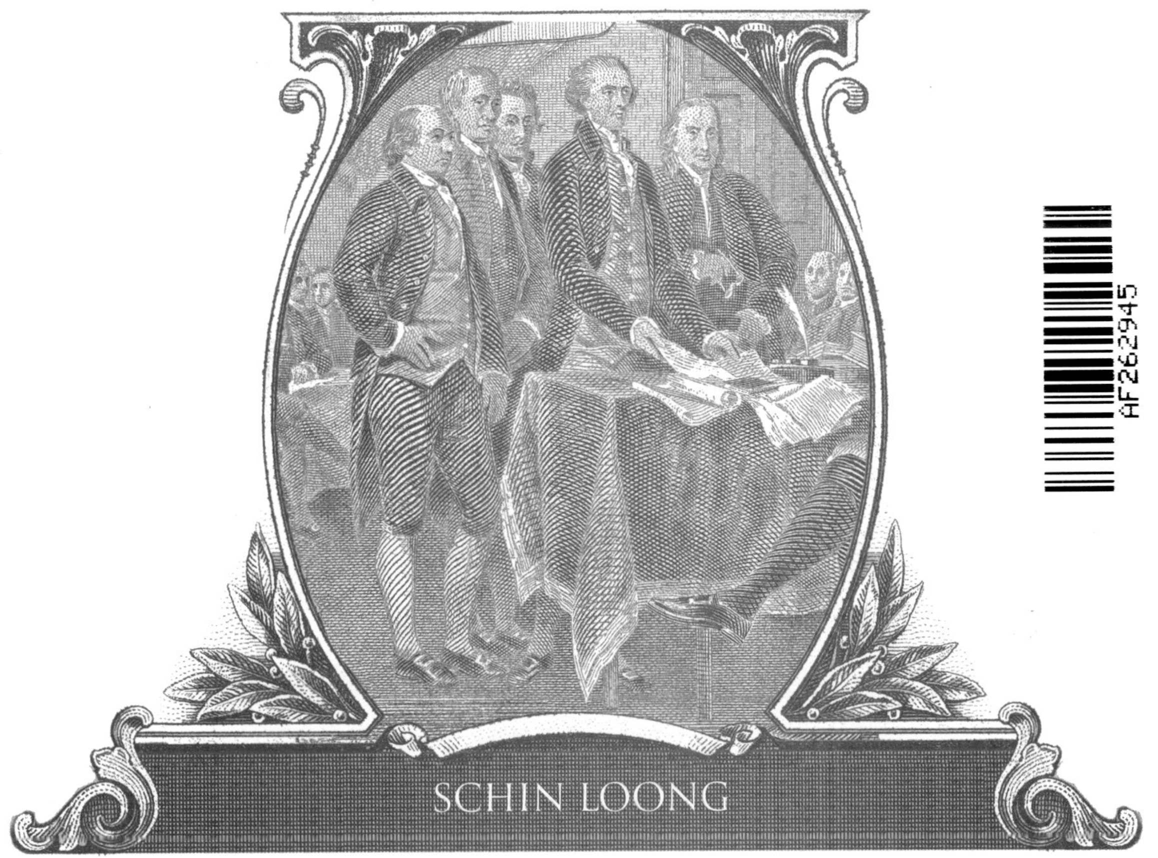

SCHIN LOONG

LEARN HOW TO WRITE LIKE THE

founding fathers

Previously published as *Spencerian Penmanship Practice Book: The Declaration of Independence*

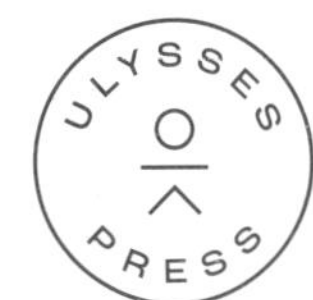

Published in 2026 by

ULYSSES PRESS

an imprint of The Stable Book Group

32 Court Street, Suite 2109

Brooklyn, NY 11201

www.ulyssespress.com

ISBN: 978-1-64604-906-6

eISBN: 978-1-64604-907-3

Managing editor: Claire Chun

Proofreader: Renee Rutledge

Cover design: Abbey Gregory

Artwork: cover Declaration of Independence © Andrea Izzotti/shutterstock.com; cover parchment © New Africa/shutterstock.com; cover quill SimoneN/shutterstock.com; founding fathers © Prachaya Roekdeethaweesab/shutterstock.com; page 5: Declaration of Independence courtesy of the National Archives

Printed in the United States

10 9 8 7 6 5 4 3 2 1

Introduction

This book is designed to make it as easy as possible for you to practice Spencerian penmanship. Across the top of each page are the words for you to practice, and below are lines, with rules and slant guides, where you can write each word again and again. You can even tear out the perforated pages to practice on a perfectly flat surface.

While the aim of this book is to improve your Spencerian script, the practice words within are not random—they are the immortal and inspiring words that Thomas Jefferson penned in The Declaration of Independence. The entire text of the Declaration can be found on the following four pages; however, in order to reduce repetition of practice words and manage the length of this book, parts of the text were not reproduced in the practice section of this book. Those parts have been underlined on the following pages.

IN CONGRESS, July 4, 1776. The unanimous Declaration of the thirteen united States of America: When in the Course of human events, it becomes necessary for one people to dissolve the political bands which have connected them with another, and to assume among the powers of the earth, the separate and equal station to which the Laws of Nature and of Nature's God entitle them, a decent respect to the opinions of mankind requires that they should declare the causes which impel them to the separation. We hold these truths to be self-evident, that all men are created equal, that they are endowed by their Creator with certain unalienable Rights, that among these are Life, Liberty and the pursuit of Happiness. That to secure these rights, Governments are instituted among Men, deriving their just powers from the consent of the governed, That whenever any Form of Government becomes destructive of these ends, it is the Right of the People to alter or to abolish it, and to institute new Government, laying its foundation on such principles and organizing its powers in such form, as to them shall seem most likely to effect their Safety and Happiness. Prudence, indeed, will dictate that Governments long established should not be changed for light and transient causes; and accordingly all experience hath shewn, that mankind are more disposed to suffer, while evils are sufferable, than to right themselves by abolishing the forms to which they are accustomed. But when a long train of abuses and usurpations, pursuing invariably the same Object evinces a design to reduce them under absolute Despotism, it is their right, it is their duty, to throw off such Government, and to provide new Guards for their future security.—Such has been the patient sufferance of these Colonies; and such is now the necessity which constrains them to alter their former Systems of Government. The history of the present King of Great Britain is a history of repeated injuries and usurpations, all having in direct object the establishment of an absolute Tyranny over these States. To prove this, let Facts be submitted to a candid world. He has refused his Assent to Laws, the most wholesome and necessary for the public good. He has forbidden his Governors to pass Laws of immediate and pressing importance, unless suspended in their operation till his Assent should be obtained; and when so suspended, he has utterly neglected to attend to them. He has refused to pass other Laws for the accommodation of large districts of people, unless those people would relinquish the right of Representation in the Legislature, a right inestimable to them and formidable to tyrants only. He has called together legislative bodies at places unusual, uncomfortable, and distant from the depository of their public Records, for the sole purpose of fatiguing them into compliance with his measures. He has dissolved Representative Houses repeatedly, for opposing with manly firmness his invasions on the rights of the people. He has refused for a long time, after such dissolutions, to cause others to be elected; whereby the Legislative powers, incapable of Annihilation, have returned to the People at large for their exercise; the State remaining in the mean time exposed to all the dangers of invasion from without, and convulsions within. He has endeavoured to prevent the population of these States; for that purpose obstructing the Laws for Naturalization of Foreigners; refusing to pass others to encourage their migrations hither, and raising the conditions of new Appropriations of Lands. He has obstructed the Administration of Justice, by refusing his Assent to Laws for establishing Judiciary powers. He has made Judges dependent on his Will alone, for the tenure of their offices, and the amount and payment of their salaries. He has erected a multitude of New Offices, and sent hither swarms of Officers to harrass our people, and eat out their substance. He has kept among us, in times of peace, Standing Armies without the Consent of our legislatures. He has affected to render the Military independent of and superior to the Civil power. He has combined with others to subject us to a jurisdiction foreign to our constitution, and unacknowledged by our laws; giving his Assent to their Acts of pretended Legislation: For Quartering large bodies of armed troops among us: For protecting them, by a mock Trial, from punishment for any Murders which they should commit on the Inhabitants of these States: For cutting off our Trade with all parts of the world: For imposing Taxes on us without our Consent: For depriving us in many cases, of the benefits of Trial by Jury: For transporting us beyond Seas to be tried for pretended offences: For abolishing the free System of English Laws in a neighbouring Province, establishing therein an Arbitrary government, and enlarging its Boundaries so as to render it at once an example and fit instrument for introducing the same absolute rule into these Colonies: For taking away our Charters, abolishing our most valuable Laws, and altering fundamentally the Forms of our Governments: For suspending our own Legislatures, and declaring themselves invested with power to legislate for us in all cases whatsoever. He has abdicated Government here, by declaring us out of his Protection and waging War against us. He has plundered our seas, ravaged our Coasts, burnt our towns, and destroyed the lives of our people. He is at this time transporting large Armies of foreign Mercenaries to compleat the works of death, desolation and tyranny, already begun with circumstances of Cruelty & perfidy scarcely paralleled in the most barbarous ages, and totally unworthy the Head of a civilized nation. He has constrained our fellow Citizens taken Captive on the high Seas to bear Arms against their Country, to become the executioners of their friends and Brethren, or to fall themselves by their Hands. He has excited domestic insurrections amongst us, and has endeavoured to bring on the inhabitants of our frontiers, the merciless Indian Savages, whose known rule of warfare, is an undistinguished destruction of all ages, sexes and conditions. In every stage of these Oppressions We have Petitioned for Redress in the most humble terms: Our repeated Petitions have been answered only by repeated injury. A Prince whose character is thus marked by every act which may define a Tyrant, is unfit to be the ruler of a free people. Nor have We been wanting in attentions to our Brittish brethren. We have warned them from time to time of attempts by their legislature to extend an unwarrantable jurisdiction over us. We have reminded them of the circumstances of our emigration and settlement here. We have appealed to their native justice and magnanimity, and we have conjured them by the ties of our common kindred to disavow these usurpations, which, would inevitably interrupt our connections and correspondence. They too have been deaf to the voice of justice and of consanguinity. We must, therefore, acquiesce in the necessity, which denounces our Separation, and hold them, as we hold the rest of mankind, Enemies in War, in Peace Friends. We, therefore, the Representatives of the united States of America, in General Congress, Assembled, appealing to the Supreme Judge of the world for the rectitude of our intentions, do, in the Name, and by Authority of the good People of these Colonies, solemnly publish and declare, That these United Colonies are, and of Right ought to be Free and Independent States; that they are Absolved from all Allegiance to the British Crown, and that all political connection between them and the State of Great Britain, is and ought to be totally dissolved; and that as Free and Independent States, they have full Power to levy War, conclude Peace, contract Alliances, establish Commerce, and to do all other Acts and Things which Independent States may of right do. And for the support of this Declaration, with a firm reliance on the protection of divine Providence, we mutually pledge to each other our Lives, our Fortunes and our sacred Honor.

In CONGRESS, July 4, 1776.

The unanimous Declaration of the thirteen united States of America,

When in the Course of human events, it becomes necessary for one people to dissolve the political bands which have connected them with another, and to assume among the powers of the earth, the separate and equal station to which the Laws of Nature and of Nature's God entitle them, a decent respect to the opinions of mankind requires that they should declare the causes which impel them to the separation. — We hold these truths to be self-evident, that all men are created equal, that they are endowed by their Creator with certain unalienable Rights, that among these are Life, Liberty and the pursuit of Happiness. — That to secure these rights, Governments are instituted among Men, deriving their just powers from the consent of the governed, — That whenever any Form of Government becomes destructive of these ends, it is the Right of the People to alter or to abolish it, and to institute new Government, laying its foundation on such principles and organizing its powers in such form, as to them shall seem most likely to effect their Safety and Happiness. Prudence, indeed, will dictate that Governments long established should not be changed for light and transient causes; and accordingly all experience hath shewn, that mankind are more disposed to suffer, while evils are sufferable, than to right themselves by abolishing the forms to which they are accustomed. But when a long train of abuses and usurpations, pursuing invariably the same Object evinces a design to reduce them under absolute Despotism, it is their right, it is their duty, to throw off such Government, and to provide new Guards for their future security. — Such has been the patient sufferance of these Colonies; and such is now the necessity which constrains them to alter their former Systems of Government. The history of the present King of Great Britain is a history of repeated injuries and usurpations, all having in direct object the establishment of an absolute Tyranny over these States. To prove this, let Facts be submitted to a candid world.

He has refused his Assent to Laws, the most wholesome and necessary for the public good. — He has forbidden his Governors to pass Laws of immediate and pressing importance, unless suspended in their operation till his Assent should be obtained; and when so suspended, he has utterly neglected to attend to them. — He has refused to pass other Laws for the accommodation of large districts of people, unless those people would relinquish the right of Representation in the Legislature, a right inestimable to them and formidable to tyrants only. — He has called together legislative bodies at places unusual, uncomfortable, and distant from the depository of their Public Records, for the sole purpose of fatiguing them into compliance with his measures. — He has dissolved Representative Houses repeatedly, for opposing with manly firmness his invasions on the rights of the people. — He has refused for a long time, after such dissolutions, to cause others to be elected; whereby the Legislative powers, incapable of Annihilation, have returned to the People at large for their exercise; the State remaining in the mean time exposed to all the dangers of invasion from without, and convulsions within. — He has endeavoured to prevent the population of these States; for that purpose obstructing the Laws for Naturalization of Foreigners; refusing to pass others to encourage their migrations hither, and raising the conditions of new Appropriations of Lands. — He has obstructed the Administration of Justice, by refusing his Assent to Laws for establishing Judiciary powers. — He has made Judges dependent on his Will alone, for the tenure of their offices, and the amount and payment of their salaries. — He has erected a multitude of New Offices, and sent hither swarms of Officers to harrass our people, and eat out their substance. — He has kept among us, in times of peace, Standing Armies without the Consent of our legislatures. — He has affected to render the Military independent of and superior to the Civil power. — He has combined with others to subject us to a jurisdiction foreign to our constitution, and unacknowledged by our laws; giving his Assent to their Acts of pretended Legislation: — For Quartering large bodies of armed troops among us: — For protecting them, by a mock Trial, from punishment for any Murders which they should commit on the Inhabitants of these States: — For cutting off our Trade with all parts of the world: — For imposing Taxes on us without our Consent: — For depriving us in many cases, of the benefits of Trial by jury: — For transporting us beyond Seas to be tried for pretended offences — For abolishing the free System of English Laws in a neighbouring Province, establishing therein an Arbitrary government, and enlarging its Boundaries so as to render it at once an example and fit instrument for introducing the same absolute rule into these Colonies: — For taking away our Charters, abolishing our most valuable Laws, and altering fundamentally the Forms of our Governments: — For suspending our own Legislatures, and declaring themselves invested with power to legislate for us in all cases whatsoever. — He has abdicated Government here, by declaring us out of his Protection and waging War against us. — He has plundered our seas, ravaged our Coasts, burnt our towns, and destroyed the lives of our people. — He is at this time transporting large Armies of foreign Mercenaries to compleat the works of death, desolation and tyranny, already begun with circumstances of Cruelty & perfidy scarcely paralleled in the most barbarous ages, and totally unworthy the Head of a civilized nation. — He has constrained our fellow Citizens taken Captive on the high Seas to bear Arms against their Country, to become the executioners of their friends and Brethren, or to fall themselves by their Hands. — He has excited domestic insurrections amongst us, and has endeavoured to bring on the inhabitants of our frontiers, the merciless Indian Savages, whose known rule of warfare, is an undistinguished destruction of all ages, sexes and conditions. In every stage of these Oppressions We have Petitioned for Redress in the most humble terms: Our repeated Petitions have been answered only by repeated injury. A Prince, whose character is thus marked by every act which may define a Tyrant, is unfit to be the ruler of a free people. Nor have We been wanting in attentions to our British brethren. We have warned them from time to time of attempts by their legislature to extend an unwarrantable jurisdiction over us. We have reminded them of the circumstances of our emigration and settlement here. We have appealed to their native justice and magnanimity, and we have conjured them by the ties of our common kindred to disavow these usurpations, which, would inevitably interrupt our connections and correspondence. They too have been deaf to the voice of justice and of consanguinity. We must, therefore, acquiesce in the necessity, which denounces our Separation, and hold them, as we hold the rest of mankind, Enemies in War, in Peace Friends. —

We, therefore, the Representatives of the united States of America, in General Congress, Assembled, appealing to the Supreme Judge of the world for the rectitude of our intentions, do, in the Name, and by Authority of the good People of these Colonies, solemnly publish and declare, That these United Colonies are, and of Right ought to be Free and Independent States; that they are Absolved from all Allegiance to the British Crown, and that all political connection between them and the State of Great Britain, is and ought to be totally dissolved; and that as Free and Independent States, they have full Power to levy War, conclude Peace, contract Alliances, establish Commerce, and to do all other Acts and Things which Independent States may of right do. — And for the support of this Declaration, with a firm reliance on the protection of divine Providence, we mutually pledge to each other our Lives, our Fortunes and our sacred Honor.

John Hancock

Button Gwinnett
Lyman Hall
Geo Walton.

Wm Hooper
Joseph Hewes,
John Penn

Edward Rutledge.

Thos. Heyward Junr.
Thomas Lynch Junr.
Arthur Middleton

Samuel Chase
Wm Paca
Thos. Stone
Charles Carroll of Carrollton

George Wythe
Richard Henry Lee
Th Jefferson
Benja Harrison
Thos Nelson jr.
Francis Lightfoot Lee
Carter Braxton

Robt Morris
Benjamin Rush
Benja. Franklin
John Morton
Geo Clymer
Jas. Smith
Geo. Taylor
James Wilson
Geo. Ross
Caesar Rodney
Geo Read
Tho M:Kean

Wm Floyd
Phil. Livingston
Frans. Lewis
Lewis Morris
Richd Stockton
Jno Witherspoon
Fras. Hopkinson
John Hart
Abra Clark

Josiah Bartlett
Wm Whipple
Saml Adams
John Adams
Robt Treat Paine
Elbridge Gerry
Step Hopkins
William Ellery
Roger Sherman
Sam el Huntington
Wm Williams
Oliver Wolcott
Matthew Thornton

Declaration of Independence

Practice Section

In Congress~ July 4,

In Congress~ July 4,

1776. The unanimous

1776. The unanimous

Declaration of the

Declaration of the

thirteen united States

thirteen united States

of America), When in the

of America), When in the

Course of human events,

Course of human events,

it becomes necessary for

it becomes necessary for

one people to dissolve

one people to dissolve

the political bands

the political bands

which have connected

which have connected

them with another, and

them with another, and

to assume among the

to assume among the

powers of the earth,

powers of the earth,

the separate and equal

the separate and equal

station to which the

station to which the

Laws of Nature and

Laws of Nature and

of Nature's God entitle

of Nature's God entitle

them, a decent respect

them, a decent respect

to the opinions of

to the opinions of

mankind requires   that

mankind requires   that

they should declare

they should declare

the causes which impel

the causes which impel

them to the separation.

them to the separation.

We hold these truths

We hold these truths

to be self-evident,

to be self-evident,

that all men are

that all men are

created equal, that they

created equal, that they

are endowed by their

are endowed by their

Creator with certain

Creator with certain

unalienable Rights,

unalienable Rights,

that among these are

that among these are

Life, Liberty and the

Life, Liberty and the

pursuit of Happiness.

pursuit of Happiness.

That to Secure these

That to Secure these

rights, Governments are

rights, Governments are

instituted among Men,

instituted among Men,

deriving their just

deriving their just

powers from the consent

powers from the consent

of the governed, That

of the governed, That

whenever any Form of

whenever any Form of

Government becomes

Government becomes

destructive of these ends,

destructive of these ends,

it is the Right of

it is the Right of

the People to alter

the People to alter

or to abolish it, and to

or to abolish it, and to

institute new Government,

institute new Government,

laying its foundation

laying its foundation

on such principles and

on such principles and

organizing its powers in

organizing its powers in

such form, as to them

such form, as to them

shall seem most likely

shall seem most likely

to effect their Safety

to effect their Safety

and Happiness. Prudence,

and Happiness. Prudence,

indeed, will dictate

indeed, will dictate

that Governments long

that Governments long

established should not

established should not

be changed for light and

be changed for light and

transient causes; and

transient causes; and

accordingly all experience

accordingly all experience

hath shewn, that

hath shewn, that

mankind are more

mankind are more

disposed to suffer, while

disposed to suffer, while

evils are sufferable,

evils are sufferable,

than to right

than to right

themselves by abolishing

themselves by abolishing

the forms to which

the forms to which

they are accustomed. But

they are accustomed. But

when a long train of

when a long train of

abuses and usurpations,

abuses and usurpations,

pursuing invariably the

pursuing invariably the

same Object evinces a

same Object evinces a

design to reduce them

design to reduce them

under absolute Despotism,

under absolute Despotism,

it is their right, it

it is their right, it

is their duty , to throw

is their duty , to throw

off such Government,

off such Government,

and to provide new

and to provide new

Guards for their future

Guards for their future

Security. Such has

Security. Such has

been the patient

been the patient

sufferance of these

sufferance of these

Colonies; and such is

Colonies; and such is

now the necessity

now the necessity

which constrains them

which constrains them

to alter their former

to alter their former

Systems of Government.

Systems of Government.

The history of the

The history of the

present King of Great

present King of Great

Britian is a history

Britian is a history

of repeated injuries and

of repeated injuries and

usurpations, all having

usurpations, all having

in direct object the

in direct object the

establishment of an absolute

establishment of an absolute

Tyranny over these

Tyranny over these

States. To prove this,

States. To prove this,

let Facts be submitted

let Facts be submitted

to a candid world. He

to a candid world. He

has refused his Assent

has refused his Assent

to Laws. He has

to Laws. He has

dissolved Representative

dissolved Representative

Houses, He has

Houses, He has

endeavoured to prevent

endeavoured to prevent

the population of these

the population of these

States ; refusing to pass

States ; refusing to pass

others to encourage

others to encourage

their migrations hither,

their migrations hither,

He has affected to

He has affected to

render the Military

render the Military

independent of and

independent of and

superior to the Civil

superior to the Civil

power. He has combined

power. He has combined

with others to subject

with others to subject

us to a jurisdiction

us to a jurisdiction

foreign to our constitution,

foreign to our constitution,

and unacknowledged by

and unacknowledged by

our laws; giving his

our laws; giving his

Assent to their Acts

Assent to their Acts

of pretended Legislation:

of pretended Legislation

For Quartering large

For Quartering large

bodies of armed troops

bodies of armed troops

among us: For cutting

among us For cutting

off our Trade with all

off our Trade with all

parts of the world:

parts of the world

For imposing Taxes on

For imposing Taxes on

us without our Consent:

us without our Consent

For depriving us in

For depriving us in

many cases, of the

many cases, of the

benefits of Trial by

benefits of Trial by

Fury: He has excited

Fury He has excited

domestic injurrections

domestic injurrections

amongst us. In every

amongst us. In every

stage of these

stage of these

Oppressions — We have

Oppressions — We have

Petitioned for Redress in

Petitioned for Redress in

the most humble

the most humble

terms: Our repeated

terms Our repeated

Petitions have been

Petitions have been

answered only by repeated

answered only by repeated

injury. A Prince

injury. A Prince

whose character is thus

whose character is thus

marked by every act

marked by every act

which may define a

Tyrant, is unfit to

Tyrant, is unfit to

be the ruler of a free

be the ruler of a free

people We, therefore,

people We, therefore,

the Representatives of

the Representatives of

the united States of

the united States of

America, in General

America, in General

Congress, Assembled,

Congress, Assembled,

appealing to the

appealing to the

Supreme Judge of the

Supreme Judge of the

world for the rectitude

world for the rectitude

of our intentions, do, in

of our intentions, do, in

the Name, and by

the Name, and by

Authority of the good

Authority of the good

People of these Colonies,

People of these Colonies,

solemnly publish and

solemnly publish and

declare, That these

declare, That these

United Colonies are, and

United Colonies are, and

of Right ought to be

of Right ought to be

Free and Independent

Free and Independent

States; that they are

States; that they are

Absolved from all

Absolved from all

Allegiance to the

Allegiance to the

British Crown, and that

British Crown, and that

all political connection

all political connection

between them and the

between them and the

State of Great Britian,

State of Great Britian,

is and ought to be

is and ought to be

totally dissolved; and that

totally dissolved; and that

as Free and Independent

as Free and Independent

States, they have full

States, they have full

Power to levy War,

Power to levy War,

conclude Peace, contract

conclude Peace, contract

Alliances, establish

Alliances, establish

Commerce, and to do all

Commerce, and to do all

other Acts and Things

other Acts and Things

which Independent

which Independent

States may of right

States may of right

do. And for the support

do. And for the support

of this Declaration,

of this Declaration,

with a firm reliance

with a firm reliance

on the protection of

on the protection of

divine Providence, we

divine Providence, we

mutually pledge to

mutually pledge to

each other our Lives,

each other our Lives,

our Fortunes and our

our Fortunes and our

Sacred Honor.

Sacred Honor.

About the Calligrapher

Schin Loong is an artist, calligrapher, and owner of OpenInkStand Studio in Las Vegas, Nevada. She holds a BFA from Ringling College of Art & Design and has 15 years of experience in combining lettering design with her distinct artistic vision. She is a member of IAMPETH (The International Association of Master Penmen, Engrossers and Teachers of Handwriting) and has studied under various master penmen, including Michael Sull, America's foremost Spencerian penman.

Other Ulysses Press Books

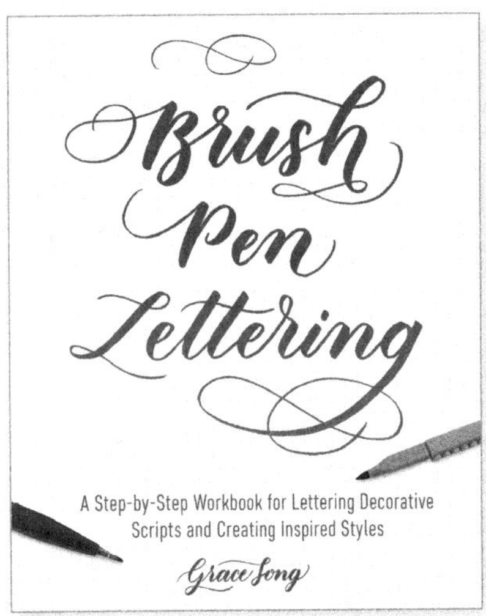

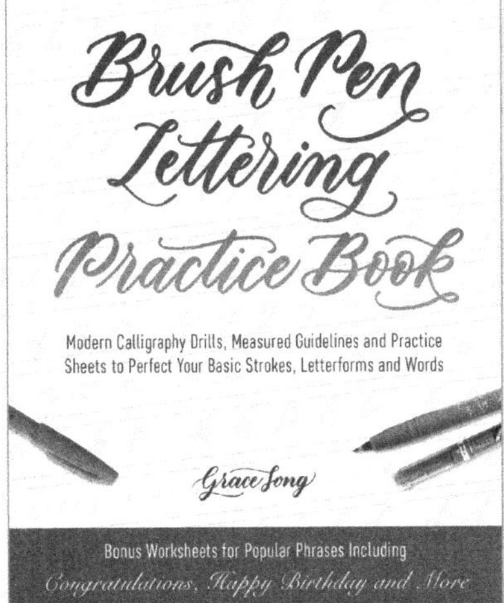

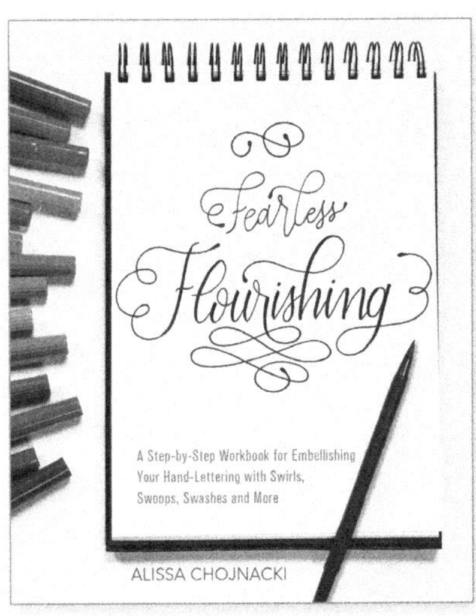

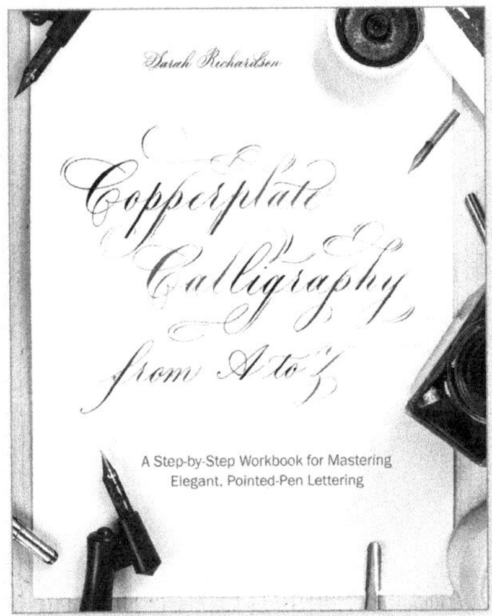

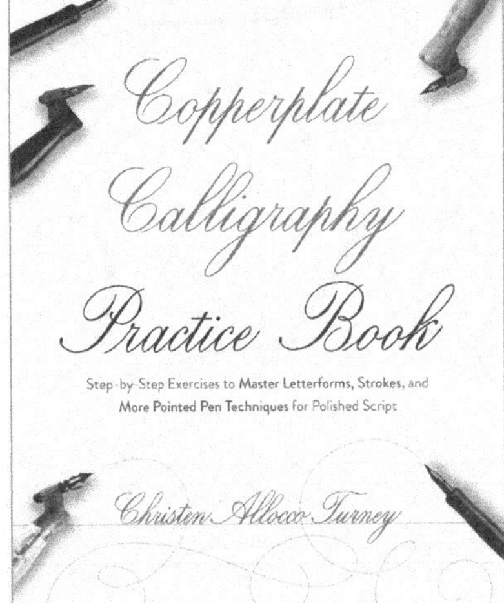

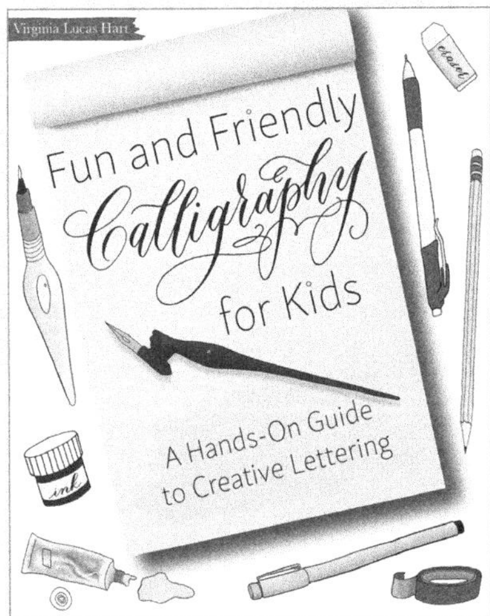

www.ulyssespress.com